101 WAYS TO BEAT THE BLUES

BY BRUCE McCULLOCH

CELEBRATE LIFE ENTERPRISES

Copyright © 1984, 2008 by Bruce McCulloch
All rights reserved
Celebrate Life Enterprises
P.O. Box 75716
Seattle, WA 98175-0716
ISBN 978-0-9793232-01
(ISBN -10) 0-9793232-0-7

Printed in the U.S.A. by Snohomish Publishing Company

I know of no more encouraging fact than the unquestionable ability of man to elevate his life by a conscious endeavor. It is something to be able to paint a particular picture, or to carve a statue, and so to make a few objects beautiful; but it is far more glorious to carve and paint the very atmosphere and medium through which we look, ... To affect the quality of the day, that is the highest of the arts.

Henry David Thoreau

Did you ever lay and listen to the rain fall?
Did you ever own a home-made apple pie?
Did you ever watch a child while he's praying?
Just don't let the Good Life pass you by.

Did you ever hold a hand to stop it's trembling?
Did you ever watch the sun desert the sky?
Did you ever hold a woman while she's sleeping?
Friend don't let the Good Life pass you by.
. . . Just took my friend there's happiness in living, somewhere between broke and being free.

As sung by Mama Cass Elliot

101 WAYS REVISITED

I first "released" 101 Ways To Beat The Blues over 20 years ago in 1984. Why reprint a simple self help book twenty some years after its first print? I just can't shake it. Every time I look at that stick figure lady jumping through a stick figure sprinkler on the back cover of the book it just lights me up. One of my friend's sisters refers to the book as 'packaged joy'. Where else can you find a stick figure bather taking a stick figure bubble bath with a 'stick figure' sign tacked to the wall in the background reading "SUCCESS IS THE PROGRESSIVE REALIZATION OF A DREAM"? I guess this reprint is simply the progressive realization of a dream.

And I couldn't help but go to my bench and throw in a few substitutions. I added about seven new remedies and made the tough decision of pulling a few of my 'starters' to get some fresh legs on the floor. I figured that there was no way that I could leave "Rock out to some roots rock reggae and dance your way out of the blues" waiting in relief while "sort the socks in your sock drawer" was struggling out there. There is simply no way to feel blue when you're dipping and skanking to the soulful voice of Bob Marley.

A final note before you dive into this new edition (which is probably a first edition to most of you) don't be afraid to mix remedies and perform a couple of remedies at the same time. A double dose of remedies (rolling down a grassy hill while listening to Bob Marley's "Forever Loving Jah" for instance) will definitely pull you out of a funk. Enjoy and keep it real.

Like most people I am prone to an occasional bout of the blues. Suddenly, for no apparent reason, I will find myself sitting or laying in the same spot for hours, brooding about who-knows-what, incapable of motion or action, feeling miserable. Having no idea what brought the feeling on, I used to feel incapable of making it go away.

I have since come to realize that by performing certain very small, very simple actions, I can make the feeling go away and return to a happy functional state.

Perhaps the first and most simple of these is to take a hot shower and to sing in the shower. Without conscious intention, I began to use this as a remedy for the cyclical blues.

Before I was aware of what I was doing, I started systematically beating the blues with a large number of simple, yet effective actions - slowly spoon feeding myself a bowl of Cream of Wheat, hopping a bus and riding out the entire line, reading and re-reading my favorite children's stories.

Out of curiosity I began to write the remedies down. I found a peculiar security in keeping this collection of prescribed actions around my room. This book is an outgrowth of that collection.

Everyone one of the remedies found in this book has been road tested by myself and others, and I can say with confidence that *they do work*. But in order for them to work, you have to *actually do them*. It is not enough to simply read a description of the prescribed action.

The worst thing in the world to do when you feel blue is to lie around and wait for the feeling to go away. You will end up feeling more blue and you'll waste a lot of time. From personal experience, I can say that the blues can consume a few hours, if not half a day.

BEATING THE BLUES requires action. Each of these remedies is fairly simple to perform and most of them require only twenty minutes to half an hour (not much time compared to the hours you can spend brooding in the blues.) Yet, as simple as they are, when you are blue even the smallest task seems difficult, if not impossible. Action of any kid seems impossible. But action, simple action, is what it will take to beat the brooding. YOU MUST MAKE YOURSELF PERFORM THESE ACTIONS TO BEAT THE BLUES (or the blues will beat you.)

So when #33 says to go outside, set your sprinkler up, turn the water on full blast and run through the sprinkler, it doesn't mean to *think about* going outside and running through the sprinkler, or *imagine* what it would feel like to run through the sprinkler ("God, I haven't done that in years"); it means GO OUTSIDE, SET YOUR SPRINKLER UP, TURN THE WATER ON FULL BLAST AND RUN THROUGH THE SPRINKLER. Take control of your action, or inaction, and you take control of your moods.

If you actually do these things, you will BEAT THE BLUES. As a matter of fact, if you do all the things prescribed in this book, you will not only BEAT THE BLUES, you will enrich your life. If at the end of the next year you can say, "This year I have run through the sprinkler at least once, taught a child how to play a game, carved my initials into a fencepost, turned a room into a jungle, rolled myself down a grassy hill, written out my MASTER STRATEGIES, crouched in front of a glowing fire, written a letter to an old friend, walked barefoot around the block, taught my dog a new trick, lived in a 100% cotton sweatshirt for two days, *and* kept a Hula-Hoop under my bed which I used frequently', I can guarantee that you will have had a better year than last year.

At an early stage in my life I developed the peculiar notion that 'Life is supposed to be Fun' or 'Life is supposed to Feel Good'. I still hold to this idea. (The older a person gets, the more he will find that this notion is under heavy attack. If he is lucky, he will realize that it is an idea worth protecting and cultivating.)

From my standpoint, the quicker a person can snap himself out of the cyclical blues and start feeling good again, the better. I hope you will use these remedies to both beat the blues and enrich your life.

Sincerely,
Bruce McCulloch

Note: Although most of these remedies can be performed throughout the year, there are a few which are more summer oriented. Rather than dividing the book into seasonal sections, I trust that my reader can recognize which of the outdoor activities are best reserved for warmer days.

Some of the remedies suggested in this book involve motion or exercise. Be sure to consult your physician before attempting any vigorous form of exercise.

101 Ways to Beat the Blues

1. Take a 15 minute shower and sing as if you were performing in your first Carnegie Hall appearance.

2. Pull out a copy of your favorite children's story and read it cover to cover or read a chapter. i.e., *Tom Sawyer*, *Huckleberry Finn* or *The Secret Garden*.

3. Talk to your dog. If you don't have a dog start up a conversation with a friends pet. As a last resort go out and have a chat with the birds and squirrels.

   Remember, although dogs may not have a very extensive vocabulary - they understand a lot just from your tone of voice. Humans and dogs have a special relationship which goes back thousands of years.

4. Escape to the zoo and watch the spider-monkeys for 1/2 an hour.

5. Start planning a trip out of town, regardless of how far off your departure date is. Make a list of everything you plan to take with you. Dig out a map and use your finger to trace out your future journey.

6. Play some John Philip Sousa marches and march around your house.

7. Radically rearrange your bedroom or living room. Move your furniture around, change your wall hangings, re-locate your house plants, etc.

8. Write a letter to an old friend whom you haven't corresponded with in ages.

9. Take a hot bubble bath.

10. Prepare and serve yourself a fully balanced, highly nutritious meal (fish, vegetable, milk, bread, fruit).

Take a B-50, C-500 (milligrams) vitamin supplement, a multi-mineral supplement, two kelp tablets, and a 400 IU vitamin E supplement with your meal. You will feel much better within 20 minutes and your body will thank you for it. I've found my mood to be so dependent upon my diet that I've concluded there are two separate worlds—the world as it appears on an empty stomach (cold and intimidating), and the world as it appears after a nutritious meal. . . something to be conquered.

#10 Recipe: Here's the wonder meal which snaps me out of the blues. Take fresh cod, cut it into small strips, and drop them into a bowl which has a mixture of cider vinegar and soy sauce in it. While the fish is soaking this up, slice up some fresh zucchini and an onion. Then toss it all in a pan and cook it on medium heat, first pouring the leftover mixture of vinegar-soy sauce over the top of it. Eat this with a slice of whole wheat bread with safflower margarine, a glass of 2% milk, and a slice of cantaloupe. Take your food supplements with this and within twenty minutes you'll feel great.

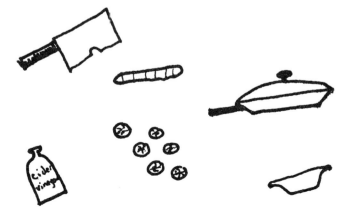

11. Go to the beach and skip rocks across the water. Go for the World's Record.

12. Make a pilgrimage to the wilderness and refresh your soul.

Hug a tree, plunge your hands into creek water, take a deep breath of clean, oxygenated air. The 'wilderness' may be a small patch of woods close to your home. Be sure to make your pilgrimage with a friend or companion – explorers rarely went it alone!

13. Build yourself a squadron of paper airplanes. Decorate each one (stars, stripes, etc.), and put a number on it. Launch them from the nearest hill, sundeck or staircase and watch them soar.

14. Paint your toenails fire-engine red. Guys too!

15. Get out of the room you're in, get out of your immediate surroundings-NOW! ABANDON SHIP!

the great escape

16. Take off your shoes and walk barefoot around the block.

17. Dig out your camera, put a fresh roll of film in it, go out and shoot a 'photo-essay' of your neighborhood.

18. Keep a Hula-Hoop under your bed at all times. When you start to feel blue, pull your Hula-Hoop out from under the bed, step into it, turn your radio on and...Hula...Hula...Hula.

Hula ... Hula ... Hula !

19. Lighten the load. Clean your closets, drawers, and storage space, and give at least 3 boxes of stuff to Goodwill. (Believe me, you won't miss a thing and you'll feel much better.)

lightening the load

20. Hop a bus and ride out the entire line.

21. Make a list of five small things which you've put off doing for at least a month...and do them; i.e., wash your car, balance your check book, water your plants.

22. Make a trip to the nearest novelty store and explore. As you examine each novelty, imagine the possible pranks you could pull and on whom you could pull them. If you can spare a few dollars, fulfill the fantasy.

My favorite is still the ole Fly-In-the-Ice Cubes. Just *think* about the utter and pointless absurdity of actually serving a guest a mixed drink with the ole Fly-In-The-Ice Cubes...Guaranteed laughter.

the 'Ole-fly-in-the-ice-cube'

(illumination, 10X)

23. Turn your radio on and tune it in to your favorite fast beat station. Crank up the volume. Grab a hairbrush, carrot or felt pen (your microphone), leap up on 'stage' and start your performance. Belt the melody into the microphone, swing your hips, leap, spin, gesticulate...give your audience a dynamite show.

up on stage

24. Set a pitcher of pure unsweetened grapefruit juice on a table with a shot glass...slam down 5 straight shots of grapefruit juice. This stuff tastes so bitter it's guaranteed to jolt you out of the blues.

It's also very good for you.

25. Read a single chapter out of a self-help book.

A couple of my favorites which I keep on hand at all times are: *The Natural Way to Super Beauty* (Mary Ann Crenshaw), and *The Magic of Believing* (Claude M. Bristol).

26. Pamper yourself with a hot bowl of Cream of Wheat with milk Put a bib on first.

27. Have somebody give you a nice looooong back massage.

28. Go on a treasure hunt – Shop thrift stores, garage sales and estate sales for 'lost' artifacts of our colorful past.

I have always been an avid garage-saler and 'thrifter' bringing home funky prints from the sixties and seventies, Zane grey books, pottery and porcelains, old pop bottles, and every sort of odds and ends. For a while I even collected old push style lawn mowers and old one speed bicycles with fat tire and wide saddle seats (much to my wife's chagrin).

'the find'

29. Make a trip to the toy store and wind up every wind-up toy they have. See how many of them you can keep going at the same time.
Be prepared to get kicked out of the store.

30. Go out and buy yourself a 100% cotton sweatshirt in your favorite color. Put it on and live in it for a couple of days.

31. Reassure yourself with the sound of your own voice...talk to yourself out loud. Give yourself a personal peptalk.

'C' mon, snap out of it pal, we've got things to do. O.K. buddy, c'mon...let's go take a hot shower and get this show on the road...that's it, now you got it...

32. Crawl under your covers with a flashlight and a very erotic piece of writing.

A recommendation? Chapter 14, *Endless Love*. There's nothing like firing up the ole hormones to pull you out of the blues.

33. Set your sprinkler up in your back yard; turn the water on full blast and 'run through the sprinkler.'

34. Start outlining your autobiography. Think up some appropriate chapter titles. Give the 'book' a name.

35. Look through your photo album and start giving the pictures captions. Print the captions clearly on little strips of paper and tape them under the pictures.

If you don't have a photo album...start putting one together.

36. Give yourself a very vigorous ten-minute scalp massage.

37. Go to your refrigerator, pull out all your leftovers and condiments and start concocting a new dish. Be reckless and inventive. When you're through, taste it and give it an appropriate name. If you feel you've discovered something, write down the recipe.

38. Take a bag of old bread down to the park and feed the ducks, pigeons, or any hugry bird or vermin.

You may not have to go all the way to the park to find a hungry bird or vermin.

39. Design and order yourself a new set of business cards – whether you're in business or not. Be sure to give yourself an outlandish title.

40. Call a used car dealer, appliance dealer, any kid of dealer, tell them you have seven hundred dollars to spend and see how long you can keep them on the phone. Make a game of it.

If there is anyone else around, grab a stopwatch and turn it into a competition.

41. Grab a basketball, bounce it down to the nearest outdoor hoop, shoot a few baskets, then bounce the ball all the way back to your front doorstep.

42. Stretch out on the grass, roll over on your back, look up at the clouds and pick out animal figures.

43. Recondition your wardrobe. Weed out all of the clothes which you don't wear anymore, and get rid of them. Take the clothes which you *do* wear and put them all back into their best possible condition. Wash, iron, dry clean, mend. Hang them neatly in your closet in wearable combinations. When you are done. . . examine your 'armoire.'

44. Spend 20 minutes grooming yourself. Brush out your hair until it shines, wash your face, floss and brush your teeth, manicure your nails.

'hanging out in the shallows'

45. Give yourself a baptism into that magical substance we call 'WATER'! Make a trip to the local pool and wade around in the shallow end of the pool.

If you can swim, crank out some laps in alternating strokes. If you can't swim – BE SURE to stay in the shallow end and consider signing up for some lessons.

46. Sit down with a fresh notebook and start forming your 'MASTER STRATEGIES'. Strategize your career...strategize your love life...strategize your life. Create some one-year plans, five-year plans, ten-year plans.

When you are done, hide the notebook in a safe spot until the next strategy session...MASTER STRATEGIES are 'TOP SECRET' material.

the Master Strategy session

47. Bundle yourself up under a pile of blankets and take a twenty-five minute nap. At the end of twenty-five minutes, jump up and start the day all over again.

48. Put on your most comfortable pair of shoes (your 'walking shoes') and go for a *very* long walk.

I recommend at least a two-to three-mile walking tour.

49. Teach a child a new game.

50. Keep a collection of Bill Cosby records around. Every time you start to feel blue, pop Cosby on the old turn table and just *try* to stay blue.

If you don't own any Bill Cosby records, I recommend you start your collection with *to russell, my brother, whom i slept with*.

51. Keep a bottle of bubble-blowing solution and a little plastic bubble blower around at all times. Every time you start to feel blue, grab your bubble blower and fill the room with bubbles. See how many bubbles you can keep in the air at the same time.

52. Call up or visit someone whom you *know* could use your help, strength or support right now and help them out.

You'll be surprised to find that by the time you get through helping another person you'll feel so good that you will forget you were ever blue.

53. Get something fixed. Repair a bicycle, mend a pair of pants, fix a leaky faucet, patch a tire, tinker with an old tape recorder. . . everyone has *something* which needs to be fixed.

If you can't seem to fix it yourself, after a good healthy try, then go ahead and call in someone or take it to someone who can.

54. Pour yourself a glass of orange juice, step outside and toast the sun. Bathe yourself in natural sunlight for at least 20 minutes.

here's to you!

55. Take a magnifying glass out to your garden and explore. Take a good look at each flower, bud, leaf, fly...take a look at the dirt. Pull up a piece of root and examine the root hairs.

I recommend a power of at least 4x but 2x will suffice.

56. Buy yourself a 64 pack of Crayola crayons and color your way through 101 WAYS TO BEAT THE BLUES.

Something magical happens when you flip open that box top and you are confronted by the visual spectacle of all 64 colors. Pull a few colors out of the box and read them before you start your artistic endeavor.

57. Sit down with a musical instrument and fill the room with 'positive vibrations'. If you don't have, or can't play an instrument, use one of the instruments we were born with to fill the room with music (whistle, hum, sing).

"Within two minutes, or even less, he had forgotten all his troubles...Not because his troubles were one whit less heavy and bitter to him that a man's are to a man, but because a new and powerful interest bore down on them and drove them out of his mind for some time...This new interest was a valued novelty in whistling...and he strode down the street with his mouth full of harmony and his soul full of gratitude." *Tom Sawyer, Chapter 1*

58. Dig through your photos and find the absolute best picture of yourself that's ever been taken. Find the negative of it. Take the negative to the nearest photo center and have it enlarged to an 8 x 10. While you're waiting for the enlargement to be processed, tack the color print on your wall. When the enlargement is ready, fit it into a beautiful frame and hang it on your wall.

59. Grab an empty coffee can and pick a bucket of berries.

60. Find a moderately sloped grassy hill. Lay down on the crest of the hill with your hands at your sides, and... roll yourself down. If one time isn't exhilarating enough for you, repeat 2-3 times.

Check the hill for rocks, sticks, and dog manure before doing this.

rolling out of the blues

61. Keep a set of fingerpaints in your house at all times and fingerpaint your way out of the blues. When you get done, mount your fingerpainting on a posterboard and hang it.

62. Start your 'people collection.'

Make a list of your favorite people. Write down the name of everybody that means any thing to you. When you've completed the list, take another piece of paper, write your name in the center, and surround it with the names from your people collection.

63. Hop on a bicycle and go on a 'tour de la city' or a 'tour de la neighborhood'. Explore some unfamiliar areas.

64. Sort your life out with the world's greatest counselor... mow your lawn.

If you don't have a lawn to mow, find someone who does.

65. Build yourself a rip-roaring fire, warm yourself in front of it, and gaze into the flames with primitive admiration.

Fire is a very big part of a man's natural history. Be sure to keep your fire enclosed in a safe certified fireplace.

66. Curl up with a good mystery, romance or adventure novel and completely lose yourself in it.

67. Take a tennis racket and a ball down to the nearest wall, backboard, garage door, cement or brick building and hit the ball against the 'wall' for at least 20 minutes. See how long you can keep your rallies going.

If you've never done this before, let me warm you that this is an *extremely* absorbing, compulsive activity. If the sun starts to go down...head for home.

68. Stretch out in an open meadow and chew on a blade of grass.

69. Take a trip to the store, bring home as many house plants as you can afford, and turn a room into a jungle.

70. Buy a sound effects record that has jungle or wilderness sounds on it (crickets, exotic bird calls, wild animal noises). When you start to feel blue, put the record on, turn off all the lights, shut all the drapes, strip yourself naked and creep around the house.

71. Start putting together a grand filing system. If you don't have a file cabinet, use cardboard boxes. Devise your own method of organizing and arranging your files. File letters, articles, newspaper clippings, photos, essays, etc. Keep a file on each of your interests.

The next time a conversation with a friend or colleague turns to one of your topics of interest, make it a point to say, "Hmm..let me pull my file on that." Make sure to keep your files up to date.

72. Teach your dog a new trick.

73. Take a large white piece of paper, and a thick felt market; in large bold print write the words,

"SUCCESS IS THE PROGRESSIVE REALIZATION OF A DREAM"

Tack it on your wall.

74. Pick up your phone, call up every friend that you have and make definite plans to see them (time, place). Make so many plans that it would be impossible to keep them all...Saturate your social calendar.

If you want to be official about it invest in an appointment book.

75. Short-sheet somebody's bed.

76. Put together a collection of positive pump-up songs. Sequence your selections in their most effective order. If you have the equipment, make a tape, or put it on your iPod.

As an example, here's the beginning sequence from my tape. *Get Down On It*, (Kool and the Gang); *You Can Get It If You Really Want*, (Jimmy Cliff); *Glory Bound*, (The Grass Roots); *Jump*, (Van Halen); *Encore*, (Cheryl Lynn).

77. Do some type of aerobic activity and work yourself into a good sweat. Get your heart working, and your blood circulating.

You may wish to join a class, or participate in a televised aerobic session. Once you get the hang of it you can start making up your own routines to music. You can use some simple jumping jacks, high kicks, etc., as a starting point. Get a book on the subject. However you do it, work yourself into a sweat and aerobicize your way out of the blues. Be sure to consult with your physician before attempting any vigorous form of exercise.

78. Pick a subject which has always intrigued you (Gypsies, Astral-Projection, International Banking); go to the library and "research it." Dig up every book you can find on the subject.

79. Using couch cushions, blankets and chairs, build yourself an 'impregnable' fort. Drag as many provisions as you can fit into the fort (popcorn, juice, magazines, a radio) and prepare for siege.

80. Root – Rock – Reggae! Listen to some reggae music and just try to keep from dipping, rocking, and skanking.

    It's impossible to feel blue while listening to this wonderful, offbeat Caribbean hybrid. Start your Root Rock collection with some Bob Marley, Jimmy Cliff, Peter Tosh, Third World, Burning Spear, or Gregory Isaacs.

81. Call up a friend and challenge them to an outdoor 'game of skill' (yard darts, badminton, croquet). Put $3.00 on the game.

high stakes yard darts

82. Go see a good "pump up" movie, i.e. Rocky, August Rush, Flashdance. Go directly from the movie theatre to a music store and purchase the soundtrack. Keep a copy of the soundtrack around at all times.

83. Choose your wild animal mascot - Be it Cougar, Bear, Wolf, Grey Whale or Big Horned Sheep, make prints of it and hang them on your wall.

    You can download images from the internet, or look through books for photos and images of these inspiring brothers and sisters who share the planet with us.

84. Keep a collection of inspirational prayers around. When you feel blue, pull them out and read them out loud to yourself.

85. Fill a pitcher with water, and a glass with water. Share a drink with your houseplants. (Be a good host and serve them first.) Talk to them, play them some music.

Keep in mind that plants *are* living creatures, have a longer natural history on this planet than animals, and are the planet's 'primary producers'—meaning *they* are the ones who convert sunlight into some consumable form of energy. You're in good company.

86. Sit down and write me a letter with your personal critique of this book. If you have any suggestions to be included in the next edition of 101 Ways to Beat The Blues be sure to include them in your letter.

My Address:
  Bruce McCulloch/Celebrate Life Enterprises
      Celebrate Life Enterprises
      P.O. Box 75716
      Seattle, WA 98175-0716

87. Go to a pet store or anywhere you can see baby animals...kittens, puppies, colts, calves...anything.

88. Look through your old magazines, cut out pictures and create a collage personalized for a special friend. Then present it to that friend.

89. Set an egg timer or alarm clock for *exactly* 30 minutes. Pick a single room in your house and see how clean you can get it before the alarm goes off. Make a game of it.

You might even want to play both announcer and contestant 'Yes, ladies and gentlemen, it's a race against the clock. . . *Oh* my God, she's got the counter wiped down and there's still 26 minutes on the clock. . . I've never seen anything like it. . . what's this, she's bringing a vacuum cleaner out with only 2 minutes on the clock. . . I can't believe this, it's never been done before. . . ladies and gentlemen *I am absolutely flabbergasted.*'

90. Pick a bouquet of fresh flowers, bring them home and arrange them.

   If it's out of season, make a trip to the store and purchase some fresh cut flowers.

91. Huddle over a steaming mug of hot tea, broth or natural cider and sip your way out of the blues.

92. Sort the socks in your sock drawer. (This may require a 5-year plan.)

93. Keep an explosive set of 'motivational tapes' around. When you start to feel blue, invite one of these dynamic speakers into your home (put the tape on) and give them your undivided attention.

I used to put these tapes down until I finally got the chance to hear one. If you've never experienced the power of great oratory, I strongly suggest you treat yourself to a 'motivational' tape. This is a subject which I have only just begun to explore, but the two most explosive tapes which I've run across are Casey Treat's BELIEVE IN YOURSELF–II, and Dave Severn's PIGS DON'T KNOW PIGS STINK.

(Casey Treat is a minister; Dave Severn is an Amway Diamond.)

94. Outline and start a complete health, self-improvement and revitalization program. Imagine that you're going to turn yourself into SUPERMAN or SUPERWOMAN.

Devise your personal exercise and nutritional program (with food supplements). Make up a chart. Make a list of 'SUPERFOODS'. (This may require a little research.)

95. Plant a vegetable garden. Pop some pea, radish, lettuce, or Swiss Chard seeds into the ground and wait for them to grow.

If weather doesn't permit, or you don't have a yard, start some seeds in a window garden. Use an old egg carton as a seed starter. When the sprouts get big enough transfer them into pots and planters. Experience the power of VEGGIES!

96. Call someone whom you haven't talked to in over a year.

97. Go to the beauty or barber shop and have your hair completely re-styled, or if you can't do this immediately, do it yourself, comb your hair in a new way.

98. Wash and dry a bundle of your favorite clothes, pull them out of the dryer while they are still warm, and put them on.

99. Gather up all the borrowed items in your house, go out and return them.

This is a great 'excuse' to visit multiple friends.

100. Watch a children's sports event (soccer, Little-League baseball).

There's nothing more heart-warming than watching Little-League baseball.

101. Go out and buy 101 copies of *101 WAYS TO BEAT THE BLUES* and give them to 101 friends.